It's all about…

RIOTOUS
RAINFORESTS

KINGFISHER

KINGFISHER

First published 2015 by Kingfisher
an imprint of Pan Macmillan
a division of Macmillan Publishers International Ltd
20 New Wharf Road, London N1 9RR
Associated companies throughout the world
www.panmacmillan.com

Series editor: Sarah Snashall
Series design: Little Red Ant
Adapted from an original text by James Harrison and Claire Llewellyn

ISBN 978-0-7534-3888-6

9 8 7 6 5 4 3 2 1

1TR/0415/WKT/UG/128MA

A CIP catalogue record for this book is available from the British Library.

Printed in China

Picture credits
The Publisher would like to thank the following for permission to reproduce their material.
Top = t; Bottom = b; Centre = c; Left = l; Right = r
Cover Shutterstock/Juriah Mosin; Back cover Shutterstock/cellistka; Pages 4–5b Shutterstock/
szefel; 5 Shutterstock/Sam Chadwick; 6–7 Kingfisher Artbank; 6 Shutterstock/Arangan Ananth;
8–9 Getty/Louise Murray; 8 FLPA/Minden Pictures/Murray Cooper; 9 Shutterstock/kajornyot;
10 Shutterstock/David Havel; 11 Kingfisher Artbank; 11b Alamy/Bruce Farnsworth;
12–13 Kingfisher Artbank; 13 Shutterstock/Sebastian Janicki; 14 Shutterstock/Vadim Petrakov;
15 Kingfisher Artbank; 15t Shutterstock/Dr Morley Read; 16–17 Shutterstock/Marcos Amend;
18 Shutterstock/Ondrej Prosicky; 19b Shutterstock/Henrik Lehnerer; 19 Shutterstock/aabeele;
20–21b Naturepl/Kim Taylor; 21t Shutterstock/Dmitry Kosterov; 22 Shutterstock/Mikadun;
23 Shutterstock/macfuton; 24–25 Shutterstock/Colette3; 25t Shutterstock/outdoorsman;
25b Shutterstck/Fruzsi-Gergo; 26 Shutterstock/Fikmik; 27t Shutterstock/Michael Lynch;
27b Shutterstock/Noumae; 28–29 Shutterstock/Ja Ritnetikun; 29 Shutterstock/ZONETEEn;
32 Shutterstock/Mikadun
Cards: Front tl Shutterstock/Albie Venter; tr Shutterstock/Jiri Vaclavek; bl FLPA/Minden
Pictures/Michael & Patricia Fogden; br Shutterstock/Rich Carey; Back tl Shutterstock/
Destinyweddingstudio; tr Shutterstock/Bilal Shafi; bl Shutterstock/reptiles4all;
br Shutterstock/Mark Caunt

CONTENTS

For your free audio download go to
http://panmacmillan.com/RiotousRainforests
or goo.gl/lhp8PO
Happy listening!

Glorious rainforests

Rainforests are thick, lush forests with trees that stay green all year round. Most rainforests are tropical – they are in the hot parts of the Earth near the Equator.

FACT...

Misty rainforests called cloud forests grow high up on cool, damp mountain slopes.

The damp, warm climate is perfect for plants and wildlife. Rainforests are home to half of the plants and animals in the world.

The endangered mountain gorilla lives in the Congo rainforest.

SPOTLIGHT: The Congo

Famous for:	home of the mountain gorilla
Size:	1.5 million km²
Home to:	2000 types of animal
In danger from:	palm oil production

Lush layers

emergent layer

A tropical rainforest has four main layers. The emergent layer is the top of the tallest trees. The rainforest roof is called the canopy. Parrots, monkeys and countless other animals live here.

Leafy bushes and the tops of small trees form the understorey. The forest floor has little light and is filled with insects, ferns and dead leaves.

The tiger is hard to spot in the shadows of the rainforest floor.

canopy layer

understorey

forest floor

Life at the top

The tallest trees in the rainforest have their tops in the emergent layer. They feel the full force of the rain, the sun and the wind.

The rare harpy eagle lives in the treetops of the Amazon rainforest.

The branches of the tallest trees can spread as wide as a football pitch. They are home to soaring eagles, noisy parrots, butterflies, bats and monkeys.

Gibbons are the only apes to spend their whole lives up in the trees.

The noisy canopy

The busiest and noisiest part of the rainforest is the canopy layer. More animals live in the canopy than anywhere else in the rainforest.

The grey-headed lovebird is native to the island of Madagascar.

SPOTLIGHT: Madagascar

Famous for:	unique wildlife, including lemurs
Size:	5000 km^2
Home to:	thousands of unique animals
In danger from:	illegal logging

The canopy is home to monkeys, birds, snakes and tree frogs. Many animals can leap or glide from one tree to another.

Howler monkeys leap from tree to tree.

FACT...

Scientists build aerial walkways and fly in hot-air balloons in order to study this hidden world.

The understorey

The rainforest understorey is humid and dark. The plants that grow here have large, dark-green leaves to catch the small amounts of light.

morpho butterfly

liana

yellow-banded
poison dart frog

lobster claw plant

There is very little wind in the understorey, so plants rely on insects and animals to pollinate their flowers. There are more insects here than anywhere else in the rainforest.

This veiled chameleon likes the warm, wet conditions of the rainforest.

vine

tree frog

The forest floor

The forest floor is covered with dead leaves and twigs. These rot down and provide nutrients for the rainforest trees and plants. Tapirs and capybaras search for roots and tubers here, and it is home to small creatures such as millipedes, scorpions, spiders and earthworms.

tree frog

Capybaras are related to guinea pigs.

FACT...

Some of the largest tree trunks are four metres across – that's as wide as a medium-sized car.

The blue-wing butterfly has a very long tongue to suck up nectar from flowers.

tapir

ants

poison dart frog

buttress root

The mighty Amazon

The biggest river in the world is the Amazon. It gives its name to the Amazon rainforest – the world's largest tropical rainforest.

SPOTLIGHT: Amazon rainforest

Famous for:	the world's largest rainforest
Size:	5.5 million km^2
Home to:	millions of plants and animals
In danger from:	logging, farming, mining

The river Amazon is more than
6500 kilometres long and is home to
some amazing creatures, including
piranhas, giant catfish, electric eels,
river dolphins, manatees, caimans,
snapping turtles and capybaras.

The caiman is a fierce hunter.

Brilliant birds

More types of bird live in the tropical rainforest than anywhere else in the world. Rainforest birds can be all sizes and colours, from the tiny hummingbird to the enormous toucan.

FACT...

Hummingbirds can beat their wings 12,000 times a minute. They are the only birds that can fly backwards.

The toucan's huge beak helps the bird to keep cool.

Scarlet macaws have sharp claws for climbing.

19

Insect armies

Thousands of tiny creatures such as beetles, ants and woodlice scurry about the forest floor.

They feed on the rotting leaves and fungi. Many insects, such as ants and termites, live together in colonies that are organized like armies.

Leaf-cutter ants carry pieces of leaf back to their nest.

FACT...

Rainforest minibeasts have an important role: they break down the leaves that fall from above.

More than 50 different types of ant can live in an area of rainforest as small as half a square metre.

King of the rainforest

The beautiful jaguar prowls along tree branches in the rainforest. Jaguars search the forest floor for mice or larger animals such as monkeys, tapirs and deer.

Jaguars will even fight an alligator, and their powerful jaws can cut through a turtle's shell.

The jaguar moves very quietly on padded paws. Its spotted coat helps it to blend into the rainforest shadows.

FACT...

The jaguar is in danger of disappearing as its rainforest homes are cleared away.

The jaguar hunts monkeys, such as this squirrel monkey.

SPOTLIGHT: Jaguar

Lives:	Central and South America
Size:	about 1.5 m long
Eats:	almost any mammal
Conservation status:	threatened

Ssssnakes

Snakes are some of the deadliest animals in a tropical rainforest. Many snakes catch frogs and other small animals on the forest floor and kill them with their venomous fangs. Other snakes squeeze their victims to death.

yellow anaconda

An emerald tree boa winds its body round a branch and waits to catch its prey.

The giant Madagascan hognose snake can grow to 180 cm long.

SPOTLIGHT: Yellow anaconda

Lives:	Brazil
Size:	4 m
Eats:	birds, fish, turtles, lizards
Conservation status:	not known

Hairy and scary!

The Amazon rainforest is home to the largest spider in the world (the goliath tarantula) and the world's most venomous spider (the wandering spider).

Most tarantulas hunt rather than spin webs.

Vampire bats have very sharp teeth to bite into their prey without waking it up.

Around 1000 different types of bat live in the Amazon rainforest. They include the vampire bat, which bites into sleeping animals at night and then drinks their blood.

jumping spider

Rainforest future

Every second a piece of rainforest the size of a football field is destroyed to make a large farm, to extract minerals or to build a road. This destroys the home of countless animals and plants.

cleared rainforest

It also means there are fewer trees to take in carbon dioxide gas and give out oxygen, the gas you breathe. Too much carbon dioxide can cause global warming, when the Earth heats up.

This periwinkle grows in the rainforests of Madagascar. It is used to make medicines that treat some types of cancer.

GLOSSARY

aerial walkway A rope bridge high up in the trees.

buttress A root that grows from a tree trunk and helps the tree to stay upright.

canopy The 'roof' of the rainforest, or its layer of high branches.

carbon dioxide A gas that is released into the atmosphere.

climate The general weather in an area.

colonies Groups of animals living together.

emergent layer The tallest trees in a rainforest, above the canopy.

fungi Living things that are not plants or animals, for example mushrooms and toadstools.

global warming A rise in temperatures on the Earth.

Collect all the titles in this series!

BEASTLY BUGS
FREE Collector Cards and Downloadable Audio!

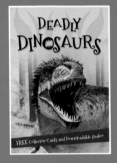
DEADLY DINOSAURS
FREE Collector Cards and Downloadable Audio!

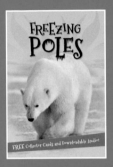
FREEZING POLES
FREE Collector Cards and Downloadable Audio!

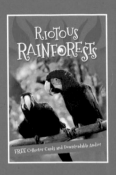
RIOTOUS RAINFORESTS
FREE Collector Cards and Downloadable Audio!

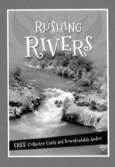
RUSHING RIVERS
FREE Collector Cards and Downloadable Audio!

SPIDERS
FREE Collector Cards and Downloadable Audio!

SNAPPY SHARKS
FREE Collector Cards and Downloadable Audio!

SUPER SOLAR SYSTEM
FREE Collector Cards and Downloadable Audio!

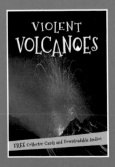
VIOLENT VOLCANOES
FREE Collector Cards and Downloadable Audio!

WILD WEATHER
FREE Collector Cards and Downloadable Audio!

INDEX

mammal An animal that feeds its young with milk from its body.

minerals Valuable substances in rocks and soil.

nutrient Food that plants and animals need to take in so they can grow.

pollinate To transfer pollen from one flower to another, so that a new plant can grow.

prey Animals hunted for food.

tropical Describes warm places near the hottest part of the Equator.

tuber The swollen stem of a plant, which grows underground.

understorey The area above the forest floor where bushes and young trees grow close together.